To our very good
Bridie and Hugh.(?)
for your kindness, frequent hospitality
and many, many laughs and good craic!
John & Mel.   August 2019

BOTH BRITTLE AND BEAUTIFUL

POEMS BY JOHN TROTMAN

Great to see you here on the island.
Come back soon! J.

R Trotman

Shanklin.

In memory of my parents
Campbell and Audrey Trotman

Cover painting:
Downstream Looking towards Gasometer 1
By Day Bowman

MOAT SOLE PUBLISHING

17 Wheelwrights Way, Eastry, Sandwich, Kent CT13 0JT

First Published by Moat Sole Publishing, 2015
Copyright © John Trotman, 2015
The moral right of the author has been asserted

A CIP catalogue record for this book is available from The British Library

Paperback: 978-0-9576925-3-4   Kindle: 978-0-9576925-4-1
ePub: 978-0-9576925-5-8

Design by Moat Sole Publishing
Printed in the UK by 4edge Limited

BOTH BRITTLE AND BEAUTIFUL

Both Brittle And Beautiful

"Both brittle and beautiful", from exhibition notes on
paintings by Day Bowman: the Gasometer series in
the Exhibition 'Urban Wastelands'

Heroic once, these visionary towers
born in geometry: clean lines, sharp,
crisp, precise, measured, ruled and neat.
Translated into steel and iron, cast
and machined; fine tolerance. Hard
rivet.
Bolt.
Weld.
Screw.
Tight.
Fixed.
Solid.
Tough.
Steel gasometer, sheer bulk against
the sky, riding pressured vapour
a piston, smooth and strong.

But for entropy.

Steel is merely
skin,
cracking
sloughed off
exfoliated
abraded
pores and scabs
of flaking rust.

Falling.

In Bowman's pictures is time:
the sharp and clean and strong
is scumbled
smudged
rubbed

scribbled
scoured
splashed
and blurred.
And with decay comes colour:
rust's orange,
like fungus flecks
mustard stain
soured cream.

Metal becomes organic.

Rots.

The Shadow Plane

I watched the shadow plane again and again
Disappear into the glass face, emerging, transformed
As ballooning fireball, orange, red and black.
Again and again trailing oily columns from the north tower
Presaged the same plane shadow, the bright billow
Suck of air, dragging smoke.
The morning bright and clear, the buildings sheer
Soaring. Silver-flashing glass.
The ticking clock, engines screaming, near......

Last night, as I watched Swan Lake, death was gathering in the wings.
This morning, Sebastian played Debussy: 'Reflections on the Water'.
On The Hudson River night lights will have shimmered.
Here, the sun shone. A pupil made us laugh, staggering across the lawn
The stars and stripes, his painting, enormous hardboard in his arms.

'Holy shit!'
Holy shit.
New York drains Inspector, caught on tape
His spot on, breathless, wondering cry.
From below, we watched with him the first impact:
The plane, an arrow streaking steady to its mark, its cargo
Fear, fuel and passion. Steel. And bitter history.

And as the day went on there came on other films
Photographs, perspectives. So several dozen planes
Were moving, irresistible
As if to prove the dream were true.
Feeding birds plunging, deadly, into a glassy sea.
Dots, human, falling slowly from the sky.
Paper surging on the black gusts
Bright flame. Again. Again.

And dust.
How structures, silver white and glass, from which
I gazed two weeks before, were
Suddenly grey dust pouring: a magic trick.
Surging, a pumice waterfall full spate
Rushing to the canyon floor below.

A hurrying cloud, last seen in fierce volcano films
Rolling (such energy!) upon cameras, cars
Stunned staff of offices
City traders, firemen, suits and secretaries.
Day's brilliance engulfed in acrid darkness,
A cloud of bitter horror drifting through the dream city.
Liberty's raised arm and torch, across the water
Copper green, faint now, smudging in gathering gloom.

Then suddenly Carol was there, from Boston
The telephone racing her weeping words across the water
As television waves carried bright horror.
So hurt, her voice, hurting for victims, America, all humanity.
And George from Germany, 'Dad are you seeing this?'

And yes I was, we were. The dream, a bright and brilliant
Nightmare dream, was flashing round the world.

And film came through from Palestine.
They watched too.
Watched as heated girders bent and burst
As blood boiled, really, as hope choked
As hearts were breaking:

Ululation trilled the air.
And children danced.

CHOUGH.

South African Sonnets

Reflections on the Cornish chough, subject of myth and legend

(1)

In the African bush, the light bright, air crackling,
Land red, umber, bleached, burnt-brown, still,
Our tracker, Joseph, points out Bataleur's eagle, sliding
Ominous in the updraft, above the plain, the lion kill.
'Black. Red legs. Red beak,' he announces - and I am back
At once on the Atlantic coast, waves combing, rough;
Grey, flat light, turf a block of emerald, rocks wet black.
A buffeting wind. Back with the tumbling, glossy chough.
Instead of the eagle's scream, seafarer, I hear the 'kee-ow,'
Out of Arthurian mists, of the slimline acrobat,
Clinging to the western margins, dream memory now.
Even Joseph, familiar with the unfamiliar, would blink at that,
And I could smile, magisterial, then kindly speak:
'Cornish chough, Joseph. Black. Red legs. Red beak.'

(2)

Robben Island, bleak, bland and flat, lies squat and bare
Like an English wartime aerodrome, except for the fiercer grey
Chill of its maximum security prison, a single storey,
Steel doors still clanging as pilgrim tourists shuffle by and stare.
On the shore, dabbing in the shallows, African oystercatchers, their
Straight, tube beaks and legs steeped in red enamel gloss.
Mandela will have seen these often on his way to mourn his loss
In the stark and blinding quarry's glare, too tired, sometimes, to care.
Arthur, after Camlann, they say, was changed into a chough
And the Welsh talk of him sleeping, ready, in a cave,
With Sobukwe, Sisulu, Mbeki perhaps, and others of the brave,
Labouring, dreaming, as the world grumbled gently, but not enough.
Sleeping saviours of the nation, birds, waiting not dead.
Chough. Oystercatcher. Rare. Black. Red.

Layered City

Somewhere far down slips the canalised Fleet
and a dozen other branching veins, sliding
darkly brick clad to the sludged Thames
then silty creeks of Kent, Essex,
perhaps the broad grey silence of the Northern sea
or the chlorine-charcoal soak of filter beds once more.

Roman culvert
monk's ditch
chalk wall
cobbled beds of buried tracks,
oceans' rolled boulders, once shone
by cart, hoof and sandal
now layered in the clotted dark.

Curling through: the roaring, fetid Tube.
Reek of dusted, crusted oil.
Blue sparks fizz the gloom
steel lines hum through shadows,
crouch to pounce beside platforms.

Bazalgette's brick gut:
ratted restaurant fat, clogged,
heroic arches
braced against blue and yellow pressing clay.

Lead cable nerves of telephones.
Skeins of worming silicone,
glass hair filaments
flashing ones and zeros round the world.

Gas squeezed through arteries
bubbles, seeps and sourly taints.

Blackwall's Minator-roaring caverns:
clay pipes, navvies' boot and rag
remnant of tunnel collapse
pipes of cracked clay

sour concrete
chill-sweated lead.

Post Office railways wriggle
round piled foundation,
clattering.

Bunkered Cold War corridors
where stencilled signs hector
for Doomsday, lecturing the dark.

Spirals of ancient wells
steps to cellars, lost,
Blitz-sealed vaults
forgotten broken graves
a city's dripping catacombs.

Thumps
metal screams of arterial trains
angry reaming grind of moling digger
rhythmic hissing breath of shuddering lift shaft.

Saxon skull
Norman rat
Renaissance dog
matted hair and leathered skin
yellow green bones
plague pit
corpse midden.

The city's layered skins and veins
speak age, accretion:
settle, sag
renew and sag

await earth's long silence.

Leicester

Go down, go through and keep going.
The oily asphalt yields to
jackhammer's juddering blade
mechanical bucket's
scrape and chew.
Beneath is
sand
ballast
sand,
thin layers and
concrete-shrouded cable humming black.
Then the first clay
shining blue brown in the
new light,
polished by spade's slicing cut.
Soon the rasp of stone...
Excitement spreads.
Flint, chalk marl, limestone blocks.
Scrape, scrape.
Walls.
Walls emerging from the clay,
the sucking loam.
Scrape, brush, scour.
Go down - go through
and amid pebbles, leather fragments, earth:
a yellow-green-grey stub of
bone
on which the trowel snags.
Brush, coax away the clay.
Bone fragments lead to
bone length
bone hoard:
pelvis
a curling twist of spine
clavicle
skull, the jaws agape
and as days follow
the skeleton

looms through -
a king looms through.
Plantagenet.
Then clay.
Then drift
of midland sandstone,
red,
running deep.

A Defenestration and Other Prague Moments

Memories of a school visit, for John Dillistone

Muffled tinkle of snowy glass on cobble
As blade-like slivers cut the slushy air
And brush the hunched, resentful shoulders of
Our concierge. Unhurt but hurt she turns
On foreign fag-dragging decadents her
Dark, suspicious Czech or Slovak eyes to stare –
And flames......

Streets of Prague have long echoed to falling glass.
Hapless governors, Martinic, Slavata,
Sprawling in mud and midden and greenish
Shards of medieval window panes,
Then thirty years of war.

Muffled tinkle of history.

And near our anagram hotel,
Hlavkova Kolej on Jenstinska, off Reslova,
The tiny cathedral church of Cyril and Methodius;
Seat of The Metropolitan of Prague,
Where basso profundo priests were silenced
When Schmeiser bullets smacked the walls protecting
Partisans and coloured, sacred glass
Was strangely sticky red, as black jackboots
Slithered and attacked over splintered
Iconic martyrdoms, the irony quite lost.

Now, post velvet revolution, genuflecting
Businessman and fervent grandmas kiss the cross,
Then hiss in urgent unison at boisterous
Czech teenagers sheltering, thoughtless, from the
storm.
Ten years before,the furtive faithful wouldn't dare
To whisper censure, fearing other uniforms
Would soon be thronging on the stair.

In Kafka's city
Our first-heard hotel words: 'Excuse me,'
(Pittsburgh matron, jowls and purple hair and pants)
'Excuse me, I gotta move: there're insects in my room!'
Concierge - the boy this time -
Holds matron's gaze and doesn't blink
As shuffles of beetles on linoleum
Whisper down the corridor
I think.

In Kafka's city - a hospital at night -
Empty, except for shadow man in booth
Who sends us three floors up to
Silence - and more corridors, bright lights.
Beetles in a maze, we grow confused and scuttle
Until movement, kettle, behind door two twenty four.
Fevered Anglo-Persian Doshi and me, English,
In fumbling Deutsch to Korean nurse (no Czech).
The doctor types her own receipts,
The clatter scattering the shards of sense.
A babel, Kafkaesque,
While outside romanesque and gothic spires
Loom in silent sodium orange snows and
Rows of shuttered houses turn their backs.

Samson Slaying a Philistine
(about 1562) by Giovanni Bologna, called Giambologna

Victoria and Albert Museum

Sweatslick Samson
slippery ox-greased
boulder muscles
sinews
bull thighs
straddle
brace
lean
rhino wrestle
buffalo gouge.
Bone heavy limb
tight thewed
steamhammer rise
falling slam
tendon-tearing
punching rip
wrecking ball
buckling brick.
Steroid-pumped
liniment tang
blinding floodlights
spectator roar
crash tackle
jaw crack.
Prize fight smoke
spittle spatter on
lusting ringside.
Neck-stretched Philistine
clinging arm sliding
impotent on piston thigh
scrabbles in dust
gasp
blood-snot slither
sliding heels
seeking purchase
fail.

Last sight
Sundazzle
Samson shadowblack
desert sky
yellow ass teeth
grimace
whitebone slicing air.

Cruise flight.
Drone strike.

Caught in amber-trap
coldchiselled stone
death-time petrified
Samson's vengeful madstare
doomed eyes
already
seeming blind
glaring down years.
Still
pressing knee
still
omen-laden tearing hair
wielding fist describing
latent cutting arc
flash like whirr of
bladed chariot wheel
(as mincing propellor
sprays blood
on tarmac)
still
pulping blow
descending
sculpted
into
stillness
and
silent-screaming
centuries.

Sculpted

Shell, sand, salt, silt, skeleton, settle over aeons
Folding, mountains moulded press layered stone.
Quarry dynamite flashes into light white, swirl-veined marble.
Sculptor, frail flesh, grasps chill steel:
Hammer strikes metal singing, biting sharp,
Chips, chips, carves, cuts, hews
Bites cold crystal, giving birth. Pieta: eternal flesh.

Captain Oates

Oates, soldier, steps into his white void, faces front
Stooping into the hurtling night's bright storm
Bears the brunt of wind and flaying ice,
White, sharp scourings of a continent.

His mind-numbed friends stare and dream of warm
Behind the frozen billow, snap of canvas which
Swaddles each in his own descending gloom,
Vacant, impotent to raise a staying hand.

Crystal ice, the blade edge of the steel gale,
Drives against flesh already blackened, bitten,
Eyes recoiling from the knife's cold slice, but
His jaw is set, his bleak resolve firm through pain.

On a Pennine lane, secure but playing at peril,
His Antarctic epic comes to mind again:
Laughing in the blizzard, thrilled, we return to
Warmth, our little brush with wilderness enough

Yet seeing in the swirling lane a possibility,
In comfortable danger a rare rough freedom, for
Released into elemental things, simple truths appear
Something near an inheritance to make the spirit soar.

Meanwhile on screaming nights in distant Southern wastes
The ghost of the sad captain still stumbles from the door,
Crusted white in frozen, creaking gear encased
To brave his colonel God's inspecting face once more.

New Xanadu

Towers of coloured glass:
jade, shimmering bronze,
opalescent purple, ruby red,
the topmost storeys glinting
in the evening sun.
Towers against the sky
hung with spreading balconies,
ziggurat terraces, from which
cascade dark foliage
brilliant flowers: camellia
wisteria, jasmine, fine old roses
tumbling, a froth luxuriant like Capri,
like hanging Babylon or Isola Bella
lush and greenly opulent.

Winking points of candlelight flicker
on the towers, reflections dancing
from the windows and from the slipping
waterfalls and fountains which bubble,
bounce among the glass and steel,
sliding fresh and cool among these
fairy castles in the air.
The towers encircle parkland glades
and tropic forest, so ground is once again
a pristine Eden where birds fly:
the bead-like skimming blur of
hummingbird, cream white dove,
red and green of parakeet,
golden oriole, peacock blue and silver.

Transport's cruel scars, the road
and rail defiling cities of the former times,
are gone: now broad walkways
coiling stairways cool in shade
sweep about the towers' feet;
no more the wailing canyons,
petrol roar and angry hubbub of the street.
The sound about these towers now
is hum of dinner conversations hanging

in the evening air, sweet sigh of music
clink of glasses, drowsy hum of the contented hive….

And artist architect
dozing at his desk, dreams
wondrous drawings coalescing from the mist,
lunchtime's claret visions flickering
sweetly on the IMAX of the mind unblocked ……

….while Porlock planner,
pedestrian,
straightens tie.

Coughs.

Prepares to knock.

Revelations of the Inky Line
Reflections on what might have been

Professor John Milne DSC Oxen, FRS, FGS

Professor John 'Earthquake' Milne (1850-1913), the father of seismology, lived and worked for many years at Shide Hill House on the outskirts of Newport, Isle of Wight. The observatory he established in Shide became a world centre for earthquake science. To it came many visitors from all walks of life, including royalty such as Edward, Prince of Wales, Prince Galitzen of Russia and Baron Kujo, the brother-in-law of the Emperor of Japan. Captain Robert Scott spent some time with the professor and his wife before his ill-fated Antarctic expedition. Milne was awarded Japan's highest honour, the Order of the Rising Sun. A cup at the local golf club bears the name of its donor, John Milne.
(Extract from a leaflet by Quay Arts, Newport, Isle of Wight, for its exhibition 'The Art of Invention'.)

Awaiting scrutinising visit of sceptical honourable Japanese delegation
Milne, moustached, at loaded desk, sighed,
heart's beat quickening very slightly; tense
professorial tremor beneath buttoned waistcoat.

Unseen (by him)
Seismological and Unfelt Tremor Recorder (1899-1904)
jumped minutely,
pen scratching so gently,
infinitesimal inky snail trail of anxiety.

Visiting psychoanalyst, Milne's golfing friend,

blinked and saw the
Seismological and Unfelt Earth Tremor Recorder,
now weather vane of temperament, robotic diagnostician, scratch:
balanced metal arms and strung wire
clutter in corner, measuring *mood*.

And an idea dawned.

Next day at Whitecroft, proximate asylum,
patients passed down corridors unseeing
as jumping stylus tracked
neuroses in neat arcs
paranoia in peaking alpine graphs
psychosis in fierce inky scribbles
depression in dipping scooped lines:
black calligraphic hieroglyphs
upon the scrolling parchment.

Thus shaking earth and shaking souls
were bound together, as in ancient times,
by unsuspecting Shide's
scientist of shudders.

If we could but read Milne's cylinders again,
the Lost Shide Scrolls
cased in dust and crumbling down the century,
what predictive polygraphic testaments would we find?
Nascent roué, the visiting Prince of Wales'
priapic stirrings quivering the graph?
Would Russian Prince Galitzen's register
unfelt stirring of a waking proletariat?
Or Emperor's relation's vibrations hint
at Imperial Japan's Manchurian apocalypse,
the coming human quake rumbling from deep beneath?
And what of Scott, Milne's polar friend?
A prescient shiver of chill perhaps,
black shudder across the snowy white,
hint of ink freezing in chapped hands,
cupped against the fierce Antarctic gale
and sledge tracks fading.

E387

For Caroline and David Harris, hardy boat-dwellers

Themis.
Oak boards from the dark Danish woods,
where once the longships grew
to cleave the waters
and chill English hearts
by scraping up the shingle
or sinister slip onto the sand
heavy oars clunking to a stop
the war gear clattering.
Descendant Themis, E387, squatter herring boat
likewise iron clamped, tar and oakum caulked
tethered, rides the grey-green pulse,
Medina's flood and ebb
where once the splash of oars,
the billow of fat bellied sail
sent wide-eyed sentries gasping in alarm
and haring for the town.
Now this twentieth century Danish boat sits
clenched, frail and fretting above silt bank,
sighing with fatigue,
liver-spotted, age-ridden mellow hideaway
breathing comfort
but dreaming of ice floes, pitch and crash
of Bering's gales, North Seas's cutting spray
cry of gannet, fulmar and of kittiwake.
Here, now cosy Snug, the herring throngs
once thrashed the salty dark;
here behind pine panels sleeping crewmen
snored through fog banks,
winter storms and pearly dawns;
here sea boots tramped and slithered
hooked oilskins swayed
nets were hauled and shot, hauled and shot.
Ghosts of carpenter, bearded skipper, red-fisted deckhand
taciturn, tobacco-proofed, schnapps-steeped mariners
their tread heavy on the steep and narrow stair.

Ghost of callow Wehrmacht watchman too, posted like other
solitary troopers across the herring fleet
to block the traffic of hollow-eyed refugees from Europe's
nightmare.
Far from smoky Ruhr home, queasy in the rolling swell
gazing sullen at the smudged horizon
chafing for bright beer hall, Liebchen, the solid earth
as crewmen bustled, hauled and spat
grunted incomprehensible argot of the sea and shoals,
hunched shoulders, bitter, and turned their backs.

Memories tick in timbers,
creaking call of history through bulkhead, galley,
call of waves, crack of canvas, diesel clatter, wind's shriek.

Themis settles, creaks, gently, leaks,
awaits the long postponed and dreaded
slip below the slopping waves,
the seeping, tepid waters of forgetfulness.

Beach Boys

Two boys on a grey brown beach, a sand pool:
a painting by my father in a white frame.
Light swirls, Turner sea mist or snowstorm,
as the figures, my brother and me,
deft brush flesh impressions, stoop, paddle, dig.
Ribbed sand sinks and slides away under feet.
Morning wind chills skin.
Red metal spade edge rasps cruel against toe.
Blennies dart for rock shadows.
I feel crusted salt in my hair still.
The limp on hard furrows.
Later would come rough towels, the squeaking
leather of the hot car, cloying heavy smell,
wind rattling windows. Sand grains stubborn.
Mum spreading pungent butter with a biro.
Years ago.

But see my sons in the swirling paint.
Distinctive heads, movement.
Their beach. Their stoops, pool-dipping.
Sharp edge and the cut that opened,
white flap of water-corrugated skin,
sole battered in dark sand,
dripping crimson on the wet ribbed beach.
Tissues pressed, reddening, in the airless car.

Generations blurring in the silver light.
The blood line.

Seal, Suffolk

Fatty

sausage

furred grey slug

flopped on polished sand

wind in winking nostril then

flap of thalidomide limb, heave

to water edging cold strand

dips through cream salt surf

sleek torpedo

fish flash

gone.

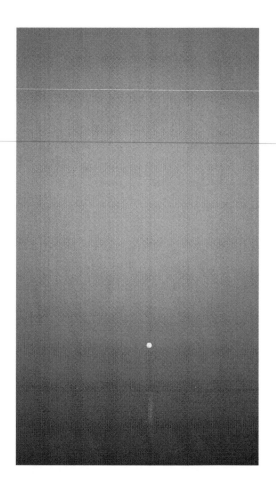

Estuary

A new moon
full tide
silted water brimming
at alders' edge
lapping sea purslane.
Reeds: clustered
resilient verticals
(suppleness their strength)
as water gathers
flows under grey light.

The estuary inhales
fills, swells before

the ebb

the sigh...

its rhythm

patterning

the days

the years.

Adventurer

The bus to school:
twisted stair, shin-cutting steel steps, lurch
and pitch, acrid dog-end reek, sweat, paper
scraps underfoot, spit. This was Real. Raw. Brave.
The bucking seats, the open back, blur of
tarmac racing away behind, the sway,
gusts and spray on the platform, rushing pavement.
Conductor a whistling adventurer,
fairground rider, bronco buster. The race
for front seat, top deck: grasp the handrail like
a vine, climb to voyeur's sight of gardens
over fences, brazen laundry, other lives.
Bedroom curtains open, glimpse of blankets
jumbled, wardrobe doors ajar. Sometimes moving
shapes. Nighties? You could hope.
High branches rushing at the windows, leaves
darkening the view suddenly in summer
with thump and scrape. Bridge bricks looming, touchable.
After Dad's car, stately, padded, swaddling, wrapped
this was the high seas, the clamber in the rigging
or the skidding mail coach clattering on the turnpike.
Closeness to rough men, rough life. Travelling.
Growing up. The thrill with me still.

I Remember

I remember the turning to the dentist's road
Down which, when my bus passed, I could not look,
Eyes scrunched, head averted to banish
For a few sweet weeks squeaking needle, grating drill,
The acrid stench and shock of burned enamel.
Almost worse to recollect, the aquarium, neon harbinger of pain
With zebra fish, bright angels, gaping guppies,
Their coiling excrement trailed beneath them, grey.
And stacked, shining, mustard-yellow National Geographics
(Winnebagoes in the Rockies, painted clapboard harbours,
Fall in Vermont, smiling check-shirted moms).
The cruel intercom would surely crackle out my name
Then mute stares of fellow patients, stairs to surgery three
And that black chair. That pink water.

Quester

In search of silver amongst sand
Prickle of perfume on desert air
Lost chord amid jangle of noise or
Bead of light in cavern's gloom
The questing soul, habituated
Pans sullen grit for ore:
Would-be lover dresses up for
Friday night again, resumes the
Modern chevalier's weary quest
His cocky courage slightly Dutch,
Garlands of faith donned and
Defiant of life's experience.
Like radio operator on storm-tossed steamer
Sinking in the howling southern seas
Who grimly combs the crackling hiss of static
Desperate for contact, human voice or morse
Refusing to leave his hopeless dials
Knowing the lapping brine is brimming
But without another plan, or course.

Sea Empress

North Sea crude, worse than just a dirty joke
defiles the salty clarity off these Pembroke shores
when Sea Empress spills and spits her bile
rasping granite with grating, plated sides.

Opened vulgar spaces yawn in her,
Kobe steel, rust, rivet and gaudy
orange red of plastered
salt resistant paint are mere cosmetic
impotent against the snagging rocks,
green and ghastly teeth on which the limpets cling,
the blenny wafts and urchins' slippery tendrils float
with popping, slithering, green-black bladderwrack
and other bobbing, pliant shapes which blur the
canine shape and strength which lie beneath.

Chinese tug (sounds like a playground game, I thought)
slithers, serious, far from home, panting in the oily foam,
strains at hawser, plaited steel line which tautens, sighs,
thread too weak to hold the yawing, fractured wall
or stem the gloss-brown fountain arching from her side.

The bruising wind buffets other victims too:
guillemot, razorbill, cormorant and shag
clogging, puzzled, in the brown and clinging acrid spew
of a wounded, bitter, Empress-hag.

And Now the Ash

Leaves of chestnut curl to crinkling claws
each midsummer as the moth takes hold,
and bleeding canker dribbles amber gouts.

Ghosts of brooding mushroom elms
haunt hedgerow, field and avenue:
Buckinghamshire, Oxfordshire, the counties stripped.

Oakwatchers weep at weeping bark
as the English heartwoods cringe. Shadows fall on
plane of city squares. Larch. Scots pine.

And now the ash, of spear and legend,
Yggdrassil, World Tree, sacred to Thor:
spores drifting on the wind, death smoke.
Leaves droop black, bark darkens. The sky cracks.

Saw-scream in the Anglian forest.
Fingers of dread curl around the heart.

So it will be now, always.

Flock

Gulls, then starlings
billowing down the evening
ballooning against sunset
gestures across darkening sky.

Always the flow of the flock
always the call of the clan
mindful of being not one
but one of the fluttering throng.

Ornithology Outing

Glimpsed, creeping at the margin of khaki reeds,
a flock in winter plumage, coats ruffled against January wind,
clustering, their cluckings, chirpings carrying
snatched fragments across the water (grey, silver).
In this winter light colours show: browns, olive, hints of green
and, looking closer, see reckless purple, still girlish pink,
sudden flash of knowing field glass.
From time to time the group disperses, clusters, strays,
individuals break off to pick at leaves, peer at tracks, faint prints,
or scan the watery horizon for smoke-swirls, eddying flocks.
At last, they gather round the dominant male, resplendent powder blue,
whose gentle call gathers the scattered crowd and leads them,
quicker now, past alder, reeds and emerald fields, to lunch.

The Butterflies

Two brown butterflies below our terrace pursue a dizzy course:
whirring electrons turning at crazy pace around an invisible
jazzing nucleus that bounces pinball-like between the trees -
a constant, wildly fluttering chase and flight, turn and weave
quick then slow and sudden nervous-quick again.

Which pursued? Then which pursuer? And as the places change
the circle's revolution changes too: clockwise now, then widdershins.
Flirtatious quarry, flirting hunter, spin and counter spin
in the morning mountain light amid the olive groves:
the eternal, vital, wearing game, which we above call love.

Two Haikus

Madam Butterfly at Sadler's Wells

Sharply shining steel
Cuts soft red silk – and blood comes
Weeping from the heart

A chill grey spring dawn
Eyes raw with lonely sorrow
Petals fluttering

Madam Butterfly

White and pink against a pearl sky
Paper screens, supple limbs
Grace and perfect measure.
Flutter of fans and almond petals
Grey dawn, a broken heart
Wailing, ancient song
And stubby, shining, ancestral steel
Cold across red silk which
Glows like blood against
Lacquer black.

Three Tankas

White, bright, lonely bird
rider of the wind's cold breath
dips to salt waves now.
Wings weary, wet feathers chill
a life's long voyage ending.

Magnolia blooms
dreamwings of pink, purple, white
April's spirit flight.
In days, wind's harsh scissors cut.
Springtime angels wince, droop, fall.

Icarus, hopeful
binds saplings, feathers; smears wax.
Desperate birdboy.
Dawn's brightening calls him skyward
freedom's warmth buoys him. Sun smiles.

Colours

Favourites, you ask. Well:
a clear, electric, magic blue in my garden: camassia leichtlinii.
Tall, spiked flowers which rise in May, but briefly
in the evening dream time when flowers' colours glow.

The deep, velvet, purple-black on some pansies
or grapes with the bloom still on them. Similar is
the stunning blue / purple / green I found last week on fresh figs.
So good.

Hard to choose the third.
The orange yellow of distant, dry-baked Atlas hills at evening.
The purple red of fuschias, rich on Ottoman carpets.
The blue of lapis lazuli (Venetian pictures of the Virgin's cloak).
The chill jade green of clear New Zealand rivers in the South.
The milky cobalt blue of lakes there too, an iced wind keening.
Or the creamy white of swans, sunlit against stormy skies.......
Terracotta in Italian sun as shadows start to creep across siesta time.....

Speckled Wood

A bleak, white-skied autumn afternoon.
Pressing against window glass
A frayed butterfly in silhouette, a speckled wood,
Patterned smudge, like lantern soot dappled
With cream dots of water drops.
Then a startled drunken bob of staggering flight
Flapping jazz dance, to settle, snared
By lightbulb's deadly welcome glow.

Within the lampshade's opaque cup
A shadow flutter, desperate
Scatter of dust and papery wing
Puny rail against confinement and horror at the heat
Until, teetering on a table top, I stretch,
Fingers gently fumbling, reaching into insect world - a god.

An Ordinary Death

A thump, a glassy rattle. A large ring of white dust flower-like on
my window. Curious, shocked, I walk to look....

Below me, on the dew-drenched grass in shadow, a pigeon trembles.
Regular shudders like heartbeat, gasps of breath, but ticking down,
his neck bent cruelly on his breast, a yellow eye quickly glazing.
The fluttering shudders slowly cease. It seems perhaps a minute,
maybe less until the eye is closed and he is nearly still. Behind
glass, warm, I gaze down as life stutters out.

Stepping into the garden, polished shoes gathering cut grass, dew,
I sense a fitting chill of clear autumnal air and stoop. So many
shades of grey in him: blue grey, white grey, dove, brown-pink
grey, a haze of grey green too about the neck, and in his wings a
charcoal, lined with white: a grey rainbow. I turn him, gently. At his
beak a thick dark blackcurrant bead of blood fills his jaws. His tiny
neck feathers splay open in rows like lapping layers pressed erect
to bare the fractured neck beneath. I spread a wing, which opens
easily, still warm, supple, though dewy grass beneath and morning
air are quickly sapping him.

I feel a sad thrill. Such terrible beauty, in that moment of his life's
end and only me to see, witness, feel for him. I reach down, caress,
a warm hand of comfort as life ebbs, then carry him gently to the
sun. Or does he only feel or fear in me the fox's jaw or cat's cruel
claw, the usual scourge of pigeons on these savage lawns?

An hour later I go again, and a small scatter of downy feathers
shows the slide toward carrion has begun again in this suburban
glade. Shadow has moved and the pigeon lies in shade once more,
as if the creeping gloom has scorned my futile effort at a sunlit
passing. His wings fan in my fingers, extending, each feather
precisely different in length and width and texture. His stiffening
claws are lobster red, grey and mustard yellow, clutching vacancy.
As I lift him into the light again, a bright, thick, trail of viscous
blood hangs down, glowing. His feathers carry brilliant, tiny
spheres of dew, which roll on the resistant down around the neck.
and the feathers' iridescence leaps in the clear light: pink like an

iceberg dawn, and the green of luminous uranium shimmering on gentle cloud. The neck flops back. His breast: mushroom? Rose? A flush of jay-like pink? Which word to catch such colour on his autumn day?

Leave him in the air. Not for him the foetid cave of refuse bin or shallow grave. The eyes will be watching from the hedges. Let them split and gnaw and take up flesh to sustain for a while their fluttering warmth and life. His beauty and spirit deserve no less, though rain comes on so soon to press all day and dissolve in darkening, shifting greys his glittering lawn and blur the shrinking earthbound shape, so soon to disappear.

The Desk

The papers pining
for attention on the desk
are mainly pitiful.
They lie there, some
limp, washed out,
routinely shunned,
still desperate
to be noticed.
Some are shy
with secrets
hidden unless
I'm vigilant, careful to
coax them open
with a little courtship –
whilst some require
a firmer hand.
These are the ruddy
fishwives, bullying
jostling and raucous
hollering dully from
the quays
reeking of
the gutting tables'
briny, bloody slop.
Others bray,
classier in that
frightful golf club way,
budding town criers
florid, self important
pushy fools,
who also want their piece of me.

Pebbles

Two hard little weights in my hand.
Smooth, both.

One matt basalt black, shunning the light
which passes not a millimetre below its secret surface
old, rolled, smoothed, by sea and sand
turned and ground, washed
and brought for just a moment to me
now.

The other a made pebble, glass.
Hard too, yet new –
water-cooled silica, brilliant bead of light
translucent, the silver rays battering through
its heart and out, bright, bursting, on the other side.

Dark and light
old and new
found and made
both holding their little piece of space, will stay;
mineral fragments of an enduring mineral universe
stones of night and day
rubbed and rolled now in my hand
warmed alike on my too transitory palm.

Two hard little weights, two hard little fickle hearts
with eons ahead - though few of them with me.
Flesh is as grass, not stone or glass.
That's tough.

Kinder Scout

On Kinder Scout
above the thronging world
of bubble and froth
a harsh wind
buffets, pressing eyes.
Tears run
salt cakes on chilling cheeks.
Peat beneath boots shines brown-black
sighs, squeaks, sags
weeps sepia after days of rain.
Whip of coarse grass.
Tugged, it rasps, cuts, though
food for haggard sheep.
Cloven prints indent the path
rank, oiled wool snags
beneath stones, clings to tufts.
Stained, grey shapes graze, shift.
Above, black rock spectres loom
as if Moore had climbed
the moor to hack, sculpt
smooth. Shapes group
bulbous against the light.
Organic, curved like flesh
rough grit, hewn
pumice to the touch.
Soil recoils, bears imprinted
impact of these great stones
giant strewn.
Sweat prickles, damp skin cools.
Neither comfortable nor comfortless:
on Kinder, a cure
where time is simple, long
wind-scrubbed
pure.

Sharp Sweetness

The colour and rich bitterness of Tuscan food
still fresh, sharp, strong and savoured in the memory:
bead-like slippery olives brown, black, green;
the shining ruddy paste, fatunta, glowing like lime
juice in its glaze of garlic and new oil;
tomatoes, salty, withered, dark-dried,
shade and shape of clotted blood;
sour, stinging saffron-green of peppers bathed in oil.
Sinewy, fat-dotted, strong salami from the wild boar
and lighter streaked prosciutto, thin and smoked to taste,
with ewes' milk cheeses white on rocket, stark and green,
their freshly shocking strengths cooled with chestnut honey
glowing gently yellow-sweet in mellow candlelight.
Crisp, white stone biscotti, hard and clean,
asparagus soft and bitter-sweet
and yellow-grey-green artichokes
unfolding secret layers to the slicing knife.
Chianti and the bloody earth of strong brunello, Montalcino's pride,
humming thick with promise in the clear-thin glass.
Coffee, thick, and serious cocoa chocolate which dries the tongue.
The beguiling rich and strong astringency which I love.

A Tuscan Quilt

Spread out across the stony hillside, a vivid Tuscan quilt:
dark oak woods raised in texture, a wool applique in rough green,
yellow vineyards in an Autumn corduroy of rhythmic ridges.
Below, studded, needlepoint of grey-green olive groves
and, running on a different grain, a patch of horizontal ancient terrace,
crumbling walls etching stripes across a scrub of background calico.
These patches, cut in rough rectangles, are stitched with lines
of dark and slender flame-shaped cypress trees and studded by
buttons of stalwart, thick-walled homes, chapels, farms.
A quilt, ancient, well-loved covering, testament to human
love and toil, through years of loyal tending and concern,
touched now at this evening moment with the slanting, golden flush
of early evening light. A gorgeous fabric on which to settle, dream.

New Zealand

Rainbow spanning copper green lake
Sparrows like locusts over lemon green willow trees
Black cattle shining in damp sunlight
Snowy peaks above the lush valley floor.

Milford : Night

Night on the Milford Track, black
soft, deep, still, with stars.....

Invisible hills loom, shapes bitten from
scattered sugar which dots the sable sky.
Tree shapes loom too, faint starlit glimmer
on thickly clustering autumn leaves.

In the cabins, ranked snorers gently snort
while others slumber on, whispering
sighing softly in the night.

Shadow moving against shadow: a waker
emerges, stands silent, then ghosts back to bed
soles softly, damply slapping on the planed timber.

Disturbed, another shape detaches from darkness:
possum, scratches, shuffling over the boarded
decking around the huts.

Orion cartwheels on the hill-horizon
the Southern Cross strong overhead.
and planets beaming.

A deepening hush.
My breath.
The stars swimming.

And a bat shape
or nightbird, flits
across my gaze

Silent, whirring
quick black
against black.

Snorer

Sleeping hut, Milford Track, New Zealand

A practised torturer, he is subtle in his horrors.
Torments come at intervals, measured pain,
Blessed respites allowing victims the illusion
Of a change of heart, compassion and release
But, terribly, the anguish could - and does - begin again.

Torture comes in outraged trumpet tones,
Like a cow robbed of her calf, lifting her great anvil
Head to the moon on lonely nights, bellowing
The loss across the starlight valley, sobbing
Echoes resounding between the darkly looming hills.

Or a stressed and stressing rending noise, like
The ripping tear an abrasive wheel repeats
On pavement slabs, as pedestrians in clouds of dust
Wince and scurry through the choking gusts
When screaming disk chews hard on grey concrete.

Then the furious roar of the Serengeti in Regent's Park
Where the slab-sided beasts bewail a chilly exile
In reeking stained grey penthouse jails;
Or the deeper, lonely, whining grunt of whales
Echoing through deep fathoms, the ocean's vacant miles.

I thrust fingers deep in ears but blood thumps
And rumbles, a coming train on the Underground.
And even so the snoring roar sounds through, a shuddering
Panicked beast on the other platform lost and raging.
The twin boomings counterpoint, competing sounds.

Other would-be sleepers sigh and shuffle, groan
Staring, I imagine, at the ceiling through the night
Zip and unzip, fingers itching as they reach
For stiletto, club, revolver, deep within their sleeping bags
Yearning for the sanctuary of the light.

At dawn, shuffling to pack, the beast is just a man,
Victim of McDonald's, Newcastle Brown.
'How was your night?' he asks, but nervously of course,
A Dr Jekyll racked with impotent remorse.
'Oh well, (I duck the question lamely) up and down….'

Sutherland Falls, South Island

Dream rhythm. A dream-inducing rhythm
as time swirls and ebbs in the surging pool.
White, hosing jets leap spitting from the stone
stark against its black, foam lace pulsing
torrents with insistent, streaming force to send
clouds, mist, spray drifting down the ferny valley.
Strong water, hard rock, soft spray.
A rainbow forever hovers, while sun shines:
glittering violet, orange, red, yellow, indigo
shimmering diamonds in the drifting gauze,
green lost against the streaming emerald cliff of moss.
From the churning column streams a wind
damply cold against cheeks, as minds pulse and drift.

As they have done for one hundred and thirty years,
whites venture, briefly, behind the crashing veil,
their cries and laughter weak amidst the water's roar.
A hundred and thirty years of awed adventurers,
just an eddy, a spurt, a watery flurry among the infinite
pulsing eddies in this island's history. Before them,
Maori: brown shadows flitting softly across the water's face.
Before them, across a dream expanse of time,
nothing, save for the flit and call of birds: tui, bell bird,
kiwi and the velvet-headed sooty robin, piping
all but inaudible as the cascade hosed and crashed.

We sit, the latest splashes on the misted lens, evaporating.

Mount Roy, Beside Lake Wanaka

On Mount Roy, looking north: light glowing in patches,
Dark ink and smudging snow clouds on Mount Aspiring,
Sunbeams struggling to slant across the darkening valley
Of Matukituki, the lake stretching in twisting steel branches
To the horizon. Below, trees are golden drops of honey.
Beside Wanaka, later, I watch water furrow, crease and rumple
In mounting wind. Willows above the narrow beach stream and strain,
Branches surging. Behind me in the flush of setting sun,
Sky is slate, salmon, metal blue, gold, clouds racing.
Tears suit in sour streets, looming cities:
Here, where the dappled, windy light slopes across Eden,
The heart is wrenched from anguish into wonder
And wind plucks bitterness from the lips.

Towards Lindis Pass

Bare Otago hills, scrubbed, rise in the clear air, coffee
Khaki, russet, olive-brown. Blue cloud shadows fold across
Their furrowed slopes like bruises, purple wine stains,
Rippling away with hawks over the dimpling gulleys.

Hills on each side rise abruptly, like clay moulded, slapped
Onto flat board, rounded mounds thrown down, smoothed
Cupped, stroked, then covered with their thin skin of
Brown ochre grass, worn and abraded by wind, patched.

Empty hills, where a climber would see and be seen below.
The fields flat, with bleached grass, during the autumn drought.
Trees in the valleys: dark, square stands of conifer,
Golden yellow, lemon and mustard lines of poplar, willow.

Lakes flat calm, of varied blue and green, opal, turquoise, milky
Cambridge blue, cobalt, slate. Chill, clear, vivid paint
Splashes across a brown canvas, with Mount Cook on the horizon,
Rearing faintly snowy blue above the clouds, against a pale sky.

Trilobite

Sun rose and set, rose and set
Sending the same shadows sliding daily across rock and sand.
Years slipping. The silence of the solid stone
Once mud, then part of layered sediment, soft seam,
Then hardening, mutating into mountain fragment.
A million years. And then a million more
Four hundred, perhaps four hundred and fifty times.
Cased in spinning rock, whirling, motionless around the sun
Carcass cast in ferrous orange stone
Now segmented body cupped within my hand
Like giant wood-louse though marine:
Curled trilobite, shrinking from the light,
From predator and from fossilising time.
Rippling waves of scuttling suppleness now
Petrified in tiny rusting-radiator-rock.
Broken open an eye blink ago, from the
Millennial cocoon-embrace of its own reflection in the mud.
Face to face with nemesis,
Now etched in indented stone.
Its twin a negative on eternity's photographic film.

Interview

Crikey! Now, you've got me there!
What's The Plan? What's now The Latest Dare?
Golly, my dear I don't have the foggiest.
Does that sound scatty? Me at my groggiest?
Well, go on admit it, you know me ,
it's just the way that I was born to be...

I like on these occasions a nice mot juste
for hacks (though you're more like a pretty Proust!)
with ticklish questions. And you ask them, I may say,
Delightfully. (A lovely dress you have on by the way....)
A neat aperçu admit it, is well within my scope;
you naughty girls expect a well turned trope
but I'm just Bumbling Boris, (yes, please put that down)
doing my best, you know? No plots, just me, the clown!

The party leader? Of course, so many ask
and as I always say, Dave is now so well up to task
and doing a splendid job, no, really splendid;
and I'm loving running London (not like Ken did!)
What a city! A real honour, a privilege!
You've seen my cosy office, by Tower Bridge?
Dave doesn't need me barging in just now
to dash the garland from his fevered brow.....
You've noticed that it's fevered? That beach blush?
Those pinched tight lips? The Flashman flush?
But he is sincere. Oh yes, I'm sure of that.
And able. Very able, I'd bet my hat.
We in Pop were sure he was officer material,
but straining p'raps for magisterial,
with a rather stunted sense of fun...
Trying just a bit hard? A little *underdone*?

But look my dear you've got me blabbing on, you know
you naughty thing. Delicious, this Moet by the way, so
absolutely de rigueur for moments just like this.
Do have a little more, it's bliss!
I must be careful not to splash it on those lovely legs again...

I have already? Clumsy bounder, what? No, it won't stain…
No, please, allow me. I insist… forgive my oafish stupor.
Gosh you have a super tan… no really, super.

'Disloyal'? Gumdrops, Paxman is a bit harsh, don't you agree…?
But then again, poor chap, he's clearly no Etonian like me!

A Fish – Eye Lens

Lines on the death of Robert Maxwell

Grey light stutters down
Through scudding waves
A timelapse glimpse
Of dawnlight skies
A slow lifting of seadepth gloom.

Brine's harsh freshness
Is now coloured
With faintest trace of swimming man
And coiling wisps of mingling oils
Sandalwood, hair oil, gin
Drift from the flailing shape against the sky.

Panic scent too.

The fish swim closer.
Soft-white, smooth-white legs
Scissor and spasm;
The struggling figure bobs
And kicks.
Fat flesh, unscaled flesh
Pitched from the roaring, churning
Distant boat.

Strength ebbs as the dawn light hardens;
Softening hairs wave
As fish mouth and nudge
The just-pulsing
White-bait-body
Before Captain Bob
Fighting Man
Clutches sea
Cries a brine and angry tear
Rolls and weeping
Sinks.

In London, duveted sons doze
Blink
Start
As faxes whine on smoked-glass desks:
'MAXWELL LOST' (Your Dad is dead)
'You're all at sea'
'You're all washed up'.

While City piranha grin and start to boil
The deeper waters
Round the Stock Exchange.

Greek Ghosts

Light and heat of the south:
olive grove and monumental fig
secret turquoise coves
scent of myrtle, oregano on rocky hillside
land where centaur and satyr trod,
priest and votress
dionysian grape-fuelled dance
to goatskin drumbeat
golden oars cutting clear waves on the trireme shore
where purple corded bales were loaded
olive oil in swaddled jars
blood warm wine, dark honey
bronze blades, leather greaves.

All down the years the hot bright
land has exhaled its history
baked limestone oozing myth and epic song.
No parched field corner, no thorny goat-dunged
scrub patch without its Attic ghosts,
pan pipes and tambourine faint behind cicada rattle.

Though now the diesels blast past
along sweating tarmac
and cola cans rattle down alleyways in a Meltemi wind
to thump of bass club rhythms
echoing round steel construction rods and stacked blocks:
still a glimpse of Aphrodite at the hotel bar
and flash of plumed helmet on the dawn-lit strand
amid the parasols; still beyond the pedalos
the ghost of galley scraping up the shingle
and Homer gazing blindly by a swimming pool.

Concert Hall

Notes of music (piano, clarinet) bubble, roll, rebound
Filling the hall, the brain, with rich re-echoing sound:
Ruby depth of woodwind, the piano's vibrant chords.
These children with such depth of music in them
Send waves of complex beauty round.
Soprano, fifteen, sings Purcell so the heart leaps:
'The Blessed Virgin's Expostulation',
Her crystal voice soaring as her hair swings.
A boy, dark eyed, sixteen, plays Brahms, an intermezzo.

Such fabric, embroidered net of notes, intricate, profound
Such subtle, poignant beauty
A sense of harmony, a sense of longing too.

What airy heights they visit with the flute, playing Reinecke,
Then the saxophone: bluesy, jazz-toned love.
And soon the orchestra crowds the stage
With Mozart: robust, rolling, rising tunes to start
Ring out, the confident assertion of a culture and a mind.
The second movement, reserved, stately, its heart hidden
But beauty there, beauty just beyond the view, waiting
Waiting to emerge from the ringing mist of sound.
Clarinet and flute dance above high strings
Before the velvet bass and cello bring a deeper tone.

But all forever ebbing, phrases falling, notes fading
Like the view behind the train, the slipping scenery
The sliding perspective of hills and farms.
Like speech, laughter, a good joke, a kiss, a look, a smile:
The music soars, then sinks. The heart is full - then pining
And permanency forever out of reach.

Moonlight Sonata

Listening to The Moonlight Sonata I thought of you,
Your voice. Honey? Velvet? Warm water? Yes, but
None of these quite: lighter, electric melancholy,
Sweet yearning, sound of wind in trees, a ripple, breath.

Bolshoi

The corps de ballet of the Bolshoi.
White arms, shoulders, hands so lithe
Like silk in the gentlest breeze
Moving, a ripple in mercury
A swan's neck dipping to its chicks.
And your ghost beside me
Your fingers gentle in my hair.

Flanders: Four Elements

Flanders earth in November rain, ploughed
Sticking, viscous, rich and sour.
'A sea of mud....,' men sighed
And furrow waves do shine,
Ripple, roll and dip to the watery
Horizon, where lines of poplars
Loom like ships through fretting spray
And greying winter air: an air that
Shivers, flaps and chills the fading day.

And fire?
That too, mainly now in cooling memory
But lurking, lurking, in the orange
Iron harvest: flaking shell and mortar dragged
From deep below, waiting, sullen
To flash and tear the air of Flanders yet again.

Earth, water, fire, air
Mixed in Flanders' long despair.
Flesh, blood, spirit, breath
Haunt these fields where farmers still
Till a land of bleeding iron and death.

11/11/11, 11a.m. Newport

The cannon's thump to sound the silence
In this island town although expected, makes
Waiting ladies near us jump and shocks
Gulls into wheeling fright, their screaming
Cries for two long minutes the only sound.
The crowd (an infant class with bright tabards,
Shivering youths and old men in car coats,
Badged berets) pauses, pensive, stirred
And, some, amused by gulls' indiscipline
Which echoes through the square where
Martial banners limply hang.

The sounds are plangent:
Island teenage soldiers crying once more
For Mum from slime of Passchendaele,
Normandy, Helmand's bitter dust,
Each cry knitting with the others down
The years into cacophony. And then
As birds' wings slowly settle the cannon cruelly
Booms to make them scream again,
Newport's soldier youth calling through the
Cries, wailing in wet November skies
To counterpoint the bugle's sad refrain.

Gas

For Tony Harrison

From secret spaces deep below
where it has bubbled, popped and seeped
through rocky centuries, filtering slow
from rot and ancient festered marsh
ferment, exhalation of earth's dead,
time's eructatious winds still blow.

Tamed and channeled, pressure standardised
it flames and flares, igniting with plosive
plop and sibilance; routes devised
pressed through pipe and metered
metronomically it warms and
cooks, illuminates to civilise.

But the ancient hissing beast lurks too
untamed, brings blinding flash
of elemental spite, a modern
belch of ancient festering gas.

Just so do ancient wrongs and hurt,
massacre and myth, diaspora
and desperate exile brew history's
weeping stinking sores, trickling
gassy poison on for years, from
beneath baked heart of Palestine
and choking still on Zyklon men
spasm in its acid stench
eyeless in Gaza once again.

Meanwhile ancient mother Russia,
flailing, hurt, belches her rockets
into a shocked and weeping sky.
And in Africa's dark heart
heirs of slaver christian, slaver moor
lock sword and scimitar once more.

Baghdad's screaming souks echo on
to roars like rampaging Tamerlane

whose pyramids of skulls presaged
modern funeral pyres and venting
inky plumes from far below, as
Sunni, Shia pack trucks with pain
peroxide, kerosene, in Allah's name.
Balkans fester on as bitter
fumes leak up through fissured limestone
and even more invisible
in sedate squares of regulated
Euro land swastikas like fate
are secretly tattooed on booted
Greek, Norwegian, French, whispering old
slogans, the flatulence of hate.

The gas is hissing still its lies:
the gorgon moves in chlorine clouds
and Baal Zebub, the ancient Lord of Flies
rots on, the insects' buzz
a drone in rising heat around
his methane-festering skull, still
staked and staring with his grinning lips
through centuries of Sinai's sun,
Still gagging for apocalypse.

RABBITTS T D S	ROOKER J H
RAESIDE W	ROPER J G
RAFTER S E	ROPER J V
RAINEY T H	ROSE C F
RALLS H	ROSE G A
RALLS H L	ROSSER E G
RANCE A G H	ROTHWELL F A
RANCE J	ROWE J W
RAND W C	ROWLAND J G A
RANDALL C W	ROWNTREE G E
RANDELL G L	ROWSELL H G
RANDELL J C	ROWTHORN P R
RAPPE L E	RUDEE R F
RAPSON S A W	RUDLAND W E
RATTLEY L S	RUNDLE A F
RAW D A	RUSSELL H F
RAWLINS B	RUSSELL J T D
RAYNER E M	RUSSELL V D
READ A F	RUSSELL W F
READ A A	RUSSELL W T
READ A T	RUSTON B T
READ R	RUTHERFORD W
REDMAN W C	RYAN A A J
REED F A	RYAN H E
REED W G	RYAN K G
REED W J	RYAN L N
REEDER G H	RYAN W G
REEDER K J	RYDER V C
REES M O	RYER R C D
REEVE C G W	SABIN P R
REEVES A J	SADLER P L
REFFLES A W	SADLER W
REID E G J	SAIT H J
REILLY J A F	SALMON W R
RENFREW L R	SALTER A J
RENNISON H W G	SALTER A J G
RENYARD C H	SALTER C H
RESTALL J E	SALTER E J
RESTELL A E	SALTER H J
REX E A	SAMMELS H C
REX E V	SAMPSON V P
REYPERT A W E	SANDERCOMBE E W
RHODES W H	SANDERSON G A
RICH S W	SANDERSON R H
RICHARDS A G	SANDFORD F W C
RICHARDS J W	SANDY J W R
RICHARDSON A C	SANGER L R
RICHARDSON G W	SANGER L V
RICHARDSON H A	SATCHELL R
RICHARDSON S A	SAUNDERS A R
RICKARD F	SAUNDERS A W
RICKARD J C	SAUNDERS F
RICKARD K H	SAUNDERS F W
RICKETTS J M	SAUNDERS J A
RIDDLE A D	SAUNDERS S J
RIDGE W	SAUNDERSON E P
RING W L	SAVAGE C J
RIPINER S E	SAVAGE F J
ROBERTON A J	SAVAGE L H
ROBERTON A W B	SAVAGE P A
ROBERTS C G	SAVINS J W
ROBERTS G A T E	SCAMMELL K E
ROBERTS G J	SCARROTT B D
ROBERTS W H	SCOTT A E
ROBERTSON J M	SCOTT A W T

Holy Isle

On granite, lead,
on white cement
or wood they wait
in squares of country towns
churchyard, county hall
cathedral cloister, office blocks
great railway stations, schools:
the lists.
Curt initials, name
and sometimes rank.
Lists.
The alphabetical dead
war's registers
the backdrop to our everydays
unread
until that November morning every year
of poppy splash
the overcoats
the bugle time.

And as 'Enigma'
drifts across the Whitehall ranks
I always think of distant Holy Isle
the single stone behind a bank
alone with sand and scudding sea
one name, one rank, one regiment:
and one sad father's words
to roll a tear on wind-chilled cheek:

'My bonny lad'.

That's all.

A Yearning

Soñando cabacea
soñando el lecho de la trilla
y soñando la muela
que hace la harina
y soñando la masa ya lluda...'

(The head nods as it dreams,
dreaming of the thresher's bed,
of the grindstone
that makes the flour,
dreaming of the risen dough..)

Miguel de Unamuno, 'La Coma Languida'

As ears of wheat, Unamuno says,
dream, yearning for the miller's
rough embrace, the steady grind
of gritstones to open and tear
the soft white heart, the rumbling
crush that man may eat

So perhaps the dusky grapes
on autumn evenings in Provence
long for treader's rhythmic stamp
to squeeze the ruby life blood
from the pulp and skin to flow
and fill the barrel, bottle, glass

And lined in row on row in
fogbound fens the ranks
of rooted onion, carrot, beet
lust in loamy dark for chef's
quick knife to flash and slice,
the fierce, ecstatic oven's flame

And beasts in sucking fields
sulk and darkly eye the enigmatic
herdsman in hope his slatted truck
will one day shudder to a stop
and they will slither up its dungy
slope, lowing in the optimistic dark

And skeins of geese in silhouette
against the leaden winter sky
croak in philosophic confidence,
call out their atavistic faith
that guns along the marsh below
will sometime sound for them.

Ordinary Fears

Night sweat and panic rising
Fear of blood swelling in the skull
Pressing brain, creeping round
The clot, the ache.
Swollen scrotum
Hanging heavy
Trembling hand and foot
Sense of sclerosis shivering through.
Deep ache below the bowel
Prostate's secret bloom.
I have feared and sensed I felt them all.
Here, mid Solent, ferry shuddering,
Rain against the windows,
Time seems short,
Which happens,
When you're sixty:
The old cliche.

David

David in his chair, bathed in lamp's soft light
Surrounded by his things and nestled from his night

Tweed tie, the many pairs of burnished chestnut shoes
Pressed suit, The Telegraph for obituary, news

Joke and anecdote, the long crossword long finished
The life beat which days and years diminished

His books of birds, the vineyards of Bordeaux,
Buckinghamshire lore, the war: to know

Those volumes was to glimpse the life.
Sculpture, the beauties hidden from his wife

And tomes on whisky, brimming with receipts
From Aberlour, Tobermory, Knockando, replete

With peaty promise of the misty glens distilled
Until, in fine thin glass his malt was swilled.

David, discreetly self possessed and quietly sage,
The gentlemanly naughty echo of a passing age.

Funeral, Perth, February 2002

Mud and rain to order.
Mudwater, a glutinous cold coffee
(we'd be drinking something similar later)
spilt across the sodden turf, squeezed out by
gravediggers' boots, then squeezed in turn by me
to settle, seeping, along the welts of
newly shining shoes, seeking out the dry.
In this slippery light, shining, too,
the coffin - sadly garish, fresh from
heated showroom. And plastic grass, new,
unrolled, bright beside the open grave.
Rain settles in trembling beads upon the
polish, crumbling dirt spattering on the gloss.
(Nana, houseproud, once would dab at that).
The minister, bishop-like in purple shirt,
is kind, in awe, he says, of three centuries
spanned by the lightweight bones we stand around.
And from the watery swishing traffic on the street
carried on the flapping air across the last Amen,
an ice cream van's tinny optimistic trill,
of Teddy Bears' picnicking in the woods.
And Dad, a little boy around his mother still,
hunches shoulders, shaking, sobs - and shakes again.

Mum : Three Memories

It was the formica table she leaned upon,
creamy yellow focus of the family kitchen.
Its legs were shaky and today so were hers,
and she wobbled that afternoon as she leaned
so sat on one of the comfortless stools:
white legs, red tops like huge buttons.
I wonder what became of them.
Mum's face in the slanting light registered fear.
She had news - and I was numb with it
before she began to speak.

I was working on a building site that Easter,
home for the vacation stacking bricks and blocks,
enjoying rawness of chapped hands and rough talk,
learning to start the thumping dumper truck
and how to keep clear of its starter handle's
casually spiteful kick on chill mornings.
Not long before the midday break, someone called me
from where I was sweeping plaster dust to clouds
in an echoing pink-brown upper room.
"Vicar's here, lookin' for you.'
My boots clumped, echoing noisily
on the naked wooden stair into the urgent daylight.
We stumbled in step across rutted ground,
past piles of empty cement and plaster sacks
ready for the fire, towards the car.
I feared for his gleaming shoes.
There were brave looking daffodils
stark in the hedge bank.
Our breath misted the windows as we drove.
He made a stab at conversation and I did too,
in a grateful way, through that long,
dazed journey to the hospital.
And then there was Dad's face, saying everything.
A strange silence.
I looked down through plate glass at a yellow crane
moving, the business of the grey afternoon going on.

Her piano had always looked astonishing,
a baby grand squeezed into our corporation sitting room.
I remember the Moonlight Sonata and Für Elise
often swelling softly from below before I slept.
The neighbours must have had to listen too.
They rarely complained, for it was beautiful,
though some fierce Brahms did prompt them once.
Each time the piano tuner came my brother and I
cowered in the kitchen, alarmed by his blind eyes
and savage, insistent striking of the keys
which made the house ring with dissonance
and reminded me a bit of Brahms, I must confess.
And when we moved, a year or so before she died,
the piano occupied a new space, but seemed huger still,
a darkly glowing polished elephant squeezed into a stable.
I don't remember her playing there; perhaps she was too sick.
And once she had gone Dad sold it quickly,
in that sadly restless, urgent way he often had.

Monica

For me it was her hair which said so much.
Immaculate, unruffled, done.
Monica: calm, self-possessed and still,
Exuding self-effacing grace. She could
Have been a gently firm headmistress
Shrewd and measured,
Measured...never rushed.
The Queen of leafy Tewin Wood.

Memory calls up dark red brick amid the green,
A house of order, calm, embodying, it seemed,
An infinite security. I remember white haired grannies,
And William of course: that fragrant pipe,
A breezy, bright inventor's Norfolk chattering laugh,
With magazines, magazines, of railways, electronics, aeroplanes;
And Bill, a drainpiped, fresh-faced Jagger, tamed:
Both kept, and kept in trim by Monica, whose patient smile,
(Only sometimes slightly strained) indulged.

We soon discovered warmth behind the measured style,
Behind precision abundant generosity.
There was bonfire night, a wedding, summer lawns,
And a time when we boys stayed the night as guests.
But it's Christmases that I remember best,
Shining golden turkeys with, mystery of mysteries,
Red, surprising-sweet Cranberry sauce.
Vivid vegetables, heaped, amid the steam,
And trifle: crimson, yellow, cream,
Layered sweet profusion
Then, minutes later, tea: mince pies,
Yuletide chocolate log, an iced and marzipanned
Snow-scened Christmas cake,
And wrapped and rustling celebration sweets:
A feast to make us sparring schoolboys drool -
Until bellies bulged and, appetites defeated,
We retreated home, replete and glowing,
Though shivering, in the chill December night.

It's hard to think of such a woman dying,
Though she has.
But somewhere rest assured she'll have a project on:
Heaven's Tupperware quickly burnished bright
She'll have that place soon tidied up and neat,
And long haired, busy angels will be sitting down
To eat!

Dad Shook

Dad shook.
He shook, lips pursed with mirth,
cheeks ruddy with delight:
the laughter rarely vocal, but bottled up and shaken
like a summer's spumante
bubbling, confined but fizzing beneath the cork.
The ridiculous or absurd,
his own jokes or recollections shared
convulsed his frame in shoulder - shaking, joyous
tremors as his eyes shone…

Dad shook.
He shook with insistent tremors, not benign
as his days drew on,
the fine painter's hands, his strongly gripping
craftsman's hands, tap tap, tap tapping,
the knife crack cracking out sudden staccatos on a
plate.

Dad shook.
He shook with sobs when family visits ended,
a sudden crumpling of the face at parting
in his latter years, wanting us to stay,
absence of Audrey and parents never far away,
his habitual sense of elegy
surging in his chest.

His often was an elegiac way -
'I'll tell you who's died' he'd say,
or, 'There's the summer gone',
his sense of life's passing shadows always strong,
knowing and loving Fitzgerald's Rubaiyat:

Dreaming when dawn's left hand was in the sky
I heard a voice within the tavern cry,
'Awake my little ones and fill the cup
Before life's liquor in its cup be dry.'

Passionate; hardly a half hearted man

Dad craved life's liquor now,
pursuing projects as the hour glass ran,
ideas realised, for him, in action,
through focus, or (the family joke) fixation.

Always active, he would do it,
discovering in Vanda a creative kindred spirit
he would make, walk, sail, ride, shoot his arrows,
play; in pencil, pen and paint he made his mark
and, teacher, loved to show the way.

An urgency in lesser actions too.
Buy it now! Make the call!
Get shot, get rid!
Now the chocolate bought (and eaten whole),
and young fermenting wine he quaffed as yeast.
Never patient, he would do:
of canoeing once he said with relish,
'around each bend always
another vista coming into view!'

And when, towards the end, when the insidious
joy-sapping tremor began its long slow shiver through
his frame
(I remember first an Italian bank, the panicked cry,
'Johnny, I can't sign my name!')
doing then was blocked, baulked, stopped up
as mum's beloved Beethoven must have known:
creative passion all pent up,
a man who did now robbed, the rider thrown.
His thwarted impulse breaking out
so he would call, cling and at times demand, I know;
when doing was denied dependency, despondency
descended.

So it was time, it was time, for Dad to go.
And the quivering struggle stilled in him.

But though he knew so well that time would carry him
away
look at the paintings to know how part of Dad will stay:

Dark figures against a yellow, snow-grey sky,

a chill Prague Spring, the spirit of Bohemia, Charles' Bridge
breathing through the paint;

The cathedral of St Vitus above, the Vlatava river
a vibrant symphony of coloured light;

Bryher Island's summer beach, wind - whipped grass
sky and sea chromatically aglow;

Venice, glittering, fragile, on its mud lagoon;

The brown and brooding stubborn bricks of Rome;

Carne, the brimming Gillan creek full of
reflected autumn light, the bright leaves turning,
soon to fall…

Beloved beasts, bleak hills and cities…

Of course the Cornish coast:
Gweek, the creeks and villages huddled to the sea
the painting subtle, strong and free;

And people in portraits – family, deeply seen and celebrated:
such mastery of touch, the character delineated.

All these mark a painter's triumph over time and tide…

and over trembling too.

Helford River

A blue December four o'clock, chill wind
gusting. Shadows lengthen as last late sunlight
slants bright across the river's wooded, sloping bank
aglow now, rising out of shadow.
Trees, stark after summer's glossy green, are orange
ochre, stripped, shivering.

The river (grey-gold, pewter, lead) is cold
stretching broad away towards its distant bend
broken only by a glistening band of silt
exposed, distinguished barely from surrounding
flood by its unbroken surface, a still
smudge set amidst water's ruffled motion
under the wind's beat.

Heron, greenshank wade the margins
and startling tippex-white egret, hunched
out of August elegance by winter's chill.
Bubbling notes of curlew, cry of gulls
and piping oystercatchers' plaintive calls
brave the wind's buffet, while below me,
where the headland's rocky prow divides the
ebbing river, two swans, mute, dip the
leaden shallows, their silent throats sinuous,
muscled, arching, bright.

Across this watery, windy space, across
the wider, greyer, wind-stripped Solent too,
across the sunset counties of the west
sinking in December's early dusk, the
electric pulses of our voices carry.
Breaths mix, lives meet and hearts beat close.
Space, water, fading light. Cold air dimming
between us, yes, a greying evening blue
but love leaps the darkening space
by phone!.....and makes it glow.

Ely

Ely: flat grey light on cathedral stone in
the fading afternoon. A late wet summer Sunday
and cloud rolls, blankets, lowering over the land again.
A tossing, damp breeze and farmers in the deadflat
fenland acres fretting now as battered harvest
musts, moulds after weeks of fitful rain. Chill creeks
channels, drains and lodes brim and spill - and our days
of lonely separation stretch away…

Inside, steadfast Norman arches bring stillness, though,
and brace the spirit. High in the crossing, around the
miracle Octagon, light slides and flutters,
subtle illumination of tracery, rib and vault.
No sound. The distant echoing steps
have ceased…the empty silence an insistent hiss
…the solitude of the soaring nave.

And suddenly, in a rush of gentle light, you are here, my little rainbow:
the nearest, massive pillar (pale chill-grey limestone)
blossoms. Spilt stains of light are scattered soft and warm.
Kaleidoscope of flushing tones: pomegranate, plum
ruby, turquoise, sunlit honey, wet lichen's
emerald, gold and harebell blue - as a rare shaft
finds the western window, painting bright the ancient
stone, once more like Ethelreda's vanished tomb
now lost, the longed for jewel at Ely's heart.

You are here: crowded meadow of Maytime flowers,
your Joseph scarf, our golden Greece.
My Rainbow Fairy. Sun. My smiling Mel. My Saxon Queen.

ACKNOWLEDGEMENTS

'South African Sonnets' were first printed in 'Chatter of Choughs', edited by Lucy Newlyn and published in 2001 by Signal Books, and in 2005 by The Hypatia Trust, in association with St Edmund Hall, Oxford.

'Estuary' was first printed in an anthology of the same name edited by Lydia Fulleylove and published by High Tide Poets, 2013.

'The Shadow Plane' was first printed in an anthology published by Bishop's Stortford College, 2001.

Cover painting and title, 'Downstream looking towards Gasometer 1', by Day Bowman (www.daybowman.com), photograph by Justin Piperger. "Chough" artist unknown. Other paintings by Campbell Trotman.

Photographs (other than photographs of John Milne and E387) by John Trotman.

With thanks to Day Bowman, Robin Ford, Joan Waddleton, Lydia Fulleylove and other members of High Tide Poets, John Dillistone, Carol Burnes, Lucy Newlyn, Quay Arts, Caroline and David Harris, my late father Campbell Trotman, Josie Chisholm, Dave Chisholm and, most of all, to my wife Mel.

John Trotman lives in Shanklin on the Isle of Wight, having moved there from Hertfordshire in 2011. He was formerly a teacher and Headmaster. He is a member of Hightide Poets at Quay Arts in Newport and a Samaritans volunteer.